CLASSROOM ACTIVATORS

64 Novel Ways to Energize Learners

D0800622

Jerry Evanski, EdD Foreword by Eric Jensen

Classroom Activators:
64 Novel Ways to Energize Learners

Jerry Evanski, EdD

 ©2004 The Brain Store®

Designer: Tracy Linares
Project Editor: Karen Graves

Printed in the United States of America
Published by The Brain Store®, Inc.
San Diego, CA, USA

ISBN #1-890460-40-0

All rights reserved. Written permission required from the publisher to use or reproduce any part of this book including the drawings, graphs, illustrations, or text except for brief quotations in critical reviews or articles.

Library of Congress Cataloging-in-Publication Data:
Evanski, Jerry
Classroom activators: 64 novel ways to energize learners
Includes biographical references and index.
ISBN: #1-890460-40-0
I. Education—Teaching.

For additional copies or bulk discounts contact:
The Brain Store®, Inc.
4202 Sorrento Valley Blvd., #B • San Diego, CA 92121
Phone (858) 546-7555 • Fax (858) 546-7560 • www.thebrainstore.com

5 7 9 10 8 6 4

Table of Contents

*A mind is a fire to be kindled,
not a vessel to be filled.*
—Plutarch

⊚ Foreword by Eric Jensen

When it comes to learning, I've always emphasized positive brain states first. Curiosity, well-being and triumph—these are three of my favorites for learning. Spark students' interest, make them feel good during your lesson and give them a chance to succeed and you'll have your audience hooked.

This little book is a big help when you are looking at learners who are slowing down, losing energy or becoming anxious, frustrated or bored. Any of the games and strategies on these pages will liven up a class immediately and excite them about coming together to learn. Every great teacher I know has a slew of activities like these in his or her back pocket. They pull one out every time they want to rescue a class going downhill or sometimes to just recapture a moment of fun.

I have used most of these classroom activators myself. Try them, tweak them and enjoy them. Remember, everything you read is backed by scientific research, educational theory and years of educational experience. The Brain Store® wouldn't have it any other way! Have fun!

⑥ Introduction

When my daughters, Julia and Emily, begin school in a few years, I want them to have kind, caring, nurturing teachers who know how to transform a classroom into a community that is free from fear and threat and rich in stimulation and support. I want them given the opportunity to share knowledge with their classmates and learn from each other. I want their teachers to know how to present curricula in ways that optimize their students' innate gifts and abilities. I also want my children to take an active role in their own learning instead of sitting quietly and passively while their instructors talk in abstractions at the front of the room.

The positive effects of such an enriched environment and the adverse effects of stress in the classroom are all well documented by research. Research also indicates that the learning brain can pay attention to a mood or item for only about twenty minutes. If something different does not occur to break the monotony, our minds start to wander. One way to eliminate the blank stares of students no longer paying attention is to vary classroom routines and refresh their brains.

Livening up the classroom atmosphere by adding variety not only brings a welcome change to a predictable day but also energizes the body, activates underutilized circuitry in the brain and helps the brain create new pathways for learning. Furthermore, activities that produce these important benefits for learning can also introduce a sense of friendly fun and interpersonal intimacy that builds community by increasing trust and support among classmates.

Luckily for you, this little book will go a long way towards helping you accomplish these goals. Each of the several dozen activators listed on these pages takes only minutes to perform, but will have a lasting positive effect on your students' attitude and learning. Whether they are performed by individuals or pairs, in small groups or with the whole class, they will enhance the spirit of teamwork and camaraderie that is so essential for creating a safe, threat-free environment where all can learn.

This book is divided into three sections. The first, *Activate Instruction*, contains suggestions and ideas for activating learning by introducing novelty and surprise to the classroom environment. The second, *Activate the Environment*, lists ideas for ways you can alter your instruction and presentation style to capture and hold student attention. The third section, *Activate Your Students*, is full of games, demonstrations, team-building exercises, ice breakers and quick physical postures that relieve the physical stress of sitting still for too long, the emotional stress of trying to learn in a room full of strangers and the instructor's stress of finding a way to transition between lessons without losing student focus! Just flip through the pages until you find an activator that intrigues you; then, try it out in your classroom. It's as easy as that.

The appropriate age range for each activator is indicated. If an activator is marked as suitable for any age, it means that I have used it successfully with students from kindergarten to adults. Be creative and modify these brain activators in any way you can imagine! By structuring your day to include active learning and peer interaction, you'll activate a new level of student energy and enthusiasm. And you'll make your classroom an exciting, enriching place to be.

Activate Instruction

Your Voice

- Change different aspects of your voice, such as tempo (how fast you speak), volume, timbre (vocal quality like nasal or falsetto) or pitch (speaking in a deep or high voice).

- Celebrity impressions get noticed—even silly, imperfect ones!

- Read with passion, really hamming it up for emotional impact.

- Laugh or tell a joke or funny story. Sing or whistle while teaching. When was the last time you did either? Try it!

- Emphasize important words, phrases or new and unusual vocabulary by slightly pausing before and after you say them, or else by speaking slowly or changing the quality of your voice for the moment. Writers use bold or italic typeface to make a point—do the same thing with your voice!

Why It Works...

Novelty drives this state change. People are hard-wired to look for and react to novelty and surprise. The brain is particularly responsive to unexpected situations during cognitive tasks (Berns et al., 1997). Use the amazing versatility of the human voice to introduce novel auditory state changes into the classroom. There is an enormous range of possibilities.

Have student be the teacher —

Your Body *opening exercises*

- If you usually stand up to teach, sit down, stand on a chair or sit or lie on the floor.

- Before you tell a story or introduce a new topic, turn your back to the audience for a few seconds to capture their interest.

- Experiment with different ways of giving directions. Write them on the board, ask a student volunteer give directions or mime them. See how long you can go without saying a word.

- Stand still. Standing perfectly still is actually quite unnatural and will be noticed very quickly.

Why It Works...

Psychologist William James (1992) suggested that we have two basic types of attention, directed (voluntary) and involuntary. Directed attention requires the brain to actively block out competing stimuli in the environment. Prolonged periods of directed attention tend to fatigue the brain's neural inhibitory mechanisms (located in the frontal lobe region), thus enabling competing stimuli to sneak into the brain's awareness. According to James, in order to keep student attention, an academic topic "must be made to show new aspects of itself." In other words, it must change. One element you can change (thereby keeping attention) is the students' visual field—what they look at. Changing your body posture or behavior is quite unexpected yet very easily accomplished.

Novelty and Surprise

The point of this state change is to have fun by deliberately doing something you ordinarily wouldn't do. What's the worst that could happen? Even if you feel silly, you'll look confident and your audience will welcome the change.

- Wear a costume to introduce an historical character or a specific period in history.

- Use props, magic tricks or unusual objects to spice up a lesson.

- Accentuate your lecture with sound effects.

- Display a mystery bag or some puzzle to solve; hide something in the room for participants to find or keep a "secret of the day" for them to guess.

- When you put a new overhead transparency on the projector, have students tap a drum roll on their desks.

- Conclude lessons and classes with teasers. For example, tell your students, "One of the greatest mysteries of mankind was found in a pyramid almost a century ago. That mystery is... the first topic we'll discuss tomorrow morning."

Why It Works...

Classrooms must contain a mix of novelty and ritual. In his seminars, Eric Jensen makes the point that too much novelty and not enough ritual leads to chaos. But too much ritual and not enough novelty leads to boredom. We love surprises! When exposed to unexpected rewards, the nucleus accumbens, an area considered the "pleasure center" of the brain, shows increased activity (Berns et al., 1997), suggesting that the element of surprise makes an experience more rewarding to the brain—and more likely to be remembered.

Choosing Volunteers

Picking a volunteer to begin an activity can also be an occasion for novelty and surprise:

■ Have students number off from one to five, but (surprise!) choose number three to go first. Or, ask partners to choose who will be "A" and who will be "B," and start with "B."

■ Designate roles rather than sequential numbers or letters for students to take within small groups. Who will be the bathtub and who will be the shower? Who will be the sunshine, lollipop or rainbow? Who will be Batman, Robin, Cat Woman or the Joker?

■ Find the person wearing the most blue and then call on the person to his right. Or, start with the person wearing the most jewelry, with the longest hair or with the biggest watch.

■ Play a tossing game to music. When the music stops, the person holding the ball answers a question.

Why It Works...

Learning accompanied by strong emotions such as excitement, mystery, surprise, joy or anticipation has a much better chance of being encoded into long-term memory. Stimulating the amygdala, which plays a crucial role in encoding and retrieving emotional memories (Cahill & McGaugh, 1998), is vital for the effective transfer of learning to long-term storage. Surprise and novelty are wonderful tools for positively changing your students' states and increasing their learning. Even choosing groups or teams in random and unexpected ways enhances team spirit and encourages better interaction among group members because of the feelings of equality it engenders (Klein & Kim, 1998; Miles & Klein, 1998).

Distribution of Resources

- Throw papers over the heads of the students, letting the papers drift down so students have to pick them up, instead of passing them out one by one.

- Hide your course syllabus or homework assignment somewhere in the room and have students locate it.

- Have a few volunteers pass out papers. Before students receive their copy, they each must compliment the person who is distributing it. Or, as a review, each student must recite a fact from the previous lesson.

- Before students receive their copy of your papers, they must first introduce to you themselves and the person sitting behind them. For example, "My name is Martha and I would like to introduce you to Beatrice."

■ Require students to tell the class a joke before they get their copy of the papers (set in advance the parameters for acceptable humor). Keep a few joke books handy for students to peruse during a break so no one is caught unprepared. Or, give one half of a joke to some students and its punch line to the others (you will need more than one joke for this variation). When they find each other, they introduce themselves and tell the joke to the class before you give them their copies of the papers.

Why It Works...

Surprise and novelty can activate emotional and attentional mechanisms in the brain to enhance learning. Researchers have examined the role of emotions by showing to college students two sets of film clips, one with emotionally charged content and one with relatively neutral content. When asked to recall details of the film clips two weeks later, the students recalled significantly more about the emotional films than the neutral films (Guy & Cahill, 1999). This message is clear: introducing novelty and surprise into the classroom is a good idea!

Feedback, Feedback, Feedback

Vary the ways your students give and receive feedback:

■ Students pick partners and re-teach what they just learned or collectively identify the three most important points of the lesson.

■ Play "Back-Words *Jeopardy*." Have students trace a one-word answer on a partner's back. The partner then supplies the question to that answer, receiving clues as necessary.

■ In small groups and to music, students toss a ball randomly around a circle. When the music stops, you ask a question. The person holding the ball must answer it for the group and the group congratulates her if she is correct, or helps her come up with the correct answer.

■ Play a short piece of music, perhaps the theme song from the *Jeopardy* game show. Before the music ends, students must write either a question they have about the lesson or a challenging question and answer pair that they will read to try to stump the class.

■ Students make a graphic organizer (such as a mind map) of what they have just learned and explain it to a partner. Alternately, they could make a partial graphic organizer and give it to a partner to complete.

Why It Works...

Students should receive some kind of feedback several times an hour! Making students wait until you return their tests and papers for feedback about their success in your course is not good brain-compatible technique.

Students learn best in an enriched environment. One of the major components of an enriched environment for human beings is immediate feedback on performance (Woodcock & Richardson, 2000). Neural pathways for new learning are solidified quickly; wrong information can be just as easily hard-wired into the brain as correct information and is very difficult to unlearn. Regular feedback can prevent having to undo incorrect learning as well as providing a fun, effective state change.

Circadian Rhythms

Change the time of day you teach different subjects in order to take advantage of biological daily rhythms. If your students routinely expect reading first thing in the morning, sometimes do math first! You could even have a backwards class; begin by giving students their homework assignment and saying good-bye, conduct the lesson, and then conclude by correcting the previous day's homework assignment and saying hello.

Backwards Day

Why It Works...

Humans have daily rhythms and cycles called circadian rhythms. Certain times of the day we naturally have more or less energy, depending on our personal cycle. If you always teach the same subject at the same time of day, you might always catch a student during the down turn of his particular circadian rhythm and never get the best out of him in that subject. Rearranging your schedule increases the likelihood that, at least once, you will teach some subject when a student is alert instead of drowsy.

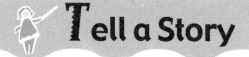

Tell a Story

Humans are natural storytellers. For untold generations, history has been handed down orally through stories. Complex ideas have been understood and explained through metaphors (think of the richness of the Greek and Roman mythologies, for example). When you need to capture your students' attention, tell them a story that ties into the subject or share a metaphor to help them better understand and internalize what you are teaching them.

Personal stories are particularly appropriate. Inspirational stories can also be found in books like *Chicken Soup for the Soul* (Canfield & Hansen, HCI, 1993). Or subscribe to a magazine like *Bits & Pieces* (Ragan Communications), which has monthly issues full of stories, anecdotes, jokes and quotes.

Why It Works...

Humans have an incredible capacity for remembering visual information. Vivid and descriptive storytelling can have a positive cognitive and emotional effect on learning (Sturm, 1999). Until students can picture in their minds what you are teaching them, they will not truly comprehend the concept. To aid memory and comprehension, wise educators experiment with stories and metaphors in their teaching, often having students create their own. Research supports the fact that imagery and emotional response are central to reading and literary comprehension (Goetz & Sadoski, 1996).

Presentation Style

Do you find yourself constantly lecturing? Once in a while, spice things up by varying your presentation style.

■ Host a guest speaker.

■ Recruit a student to teach one part of the lesson, or assign an entire lesson to a small group.

■ Show video clips or a computer slide show during your presentation.

■ Involve students more often. Have them write and perform skits, role-play, tutor each other or work together in some way. The more you can actively involve students, the better.

Why It Works...

Active involvement in the learning process is vital to the formation of new neural connections in the brain. The more an instructor can actively involve students in their own learning, the more often new knowledge will be transferred and stored in their long-term memory. Research on enriched environments reveals that active involvement is required to grow connections in the brain; it is not enough to just sit and watch something happen (Diamond, 2000)! In a study of enriched environments, an experimental group of rats lived in an environment with lots of toys, novelty, stimulation and rat companions. These rats exhibited a great deal of dendritic growth. Rats kept by themselves in cages devoid of any stimulation save the ability to observe the rats in the enriched environments showed no dendritic growth. The importance of this discovery is clear: In order to grow new connections in their brains, students must interact with their environment and each other. Sitting and listening to you lecture all day, every day, provides no opportunities to do so. Teachers must plan enrichment into their schedules.

ACTIVATE
THE
ENVIRONMENT

Lighting

- Manipulate the amount, quality and kind of light in your classroom. If you are reading a dramatic or emotional piece, shut off several banks of lights for atmosphere.

- Use dramatic lighting to tell a story. Use the overhead projector as a spotlight; shine a flashlight under your chin to light your face (remember telling scary stories around a campfire?); or have a question-answer session in the dark and point at participants with a flashlight when it is their turn to respond.

- Use table lamps instead of overhead fluorescent lighting.

- Experiment with different colors of light bulbs for holidays. Try a green bulb for Saint Patrick's Day or a red one for Valentine's Day.

Why It Works...

Our brains are hard-wired to seek novelty, perhaps as a survival instinct, to alert us to anything new in the environment so we can assess it as a potential hazard or something to ignore. Novel stimuli are not filtered out of the brain's sphere of attention. Varying the type, amount and location of lighting in a classroom can have a significant impact on a student's sense of awareness; these suggested changes of lighting are very easy ways to add novelty—and noticeability—to your lesson.

Lighting is one of the more studied aspects of educational environments. The type of lighting used in elementary classrooms may have a positive impact on student depression (Tithof, 1998) or on short-term and long-term memory and problem solving. An extensive study involving 21,000 students revealed that exposure to natural sunlight positively affects academic performance. Those students exposed to the most natural light during the day progressed 15 percent faster in math and 23 percent faster in reading than students in classrooms with the least amount of windows ("Daylighting in schools...," 1999).

Plug In

Aromas

Our sense of smell can be an immediate trigger of certain memories. Introduce certain aromas to your classroom to facilitate student learning and recall.

■ Pop fresh popcorn when beginning a new unit or reviewing for a test. Pop it again during the test.

■ Once in a while, put potpourri on your desk or on students' desks. Even a little powdered deodorizer sprinkled on the carpet will freshen the scent of the room.

■ Vanilla and lavender scents have been shown to have a positive effect on the learning environment. Read up on aromatherapy to learn about the power of other amazing essential oils when they are released into the air.

■ Instead of introducing aromas, use an air ionizer to add charged particles to the air. Ionized air occurs naturally near waterfalls or after a rainstorm. Inexpensive air ionizers can positively affect the states of your students.

Why It Works...

Research indicates that the best way to employ the benefits of aromas is to keep them in the background, barely perceptible. Interestingly, the molecules that make up the essential oils used in aromatherapy are among the few chemicals that can pass through the blood-brain barrier, which is a densely packed lining of cells that protect the brain from harmful chemicals entering the brain. Memories that are stored in the brain via multiple pathways (auditory, visual, kinesthetic or olfactory—the sense of smell) can be more easily retrieved.

Location

■ Teach your subject in another room.

■ Switch rooms with another teacher for an hour or part of a lesson.

■ Swap classes with another teacher, even for just a short while.

■ Take your students outside or into the hallway for all or part of a lesson.

■ Change where you display class notes, overhead slides or movies. Can you project onto the ceiling or another wall? Ask for a moveable chalkboard or whiteboard and move it to different locations within the room.

Why It Works...

Visual context is one of the brain's most powerful memory aids. Changing something's location not only introduces novelty and curiosity but also helps the brain remember it later. If someone asked you what you ate for dinner last Tuesday, you probably would have trouble remembering until she reminded you of the restaurant you visited. The brain more readily focuses on location than it does on other memory cues like color, hue, shape or motion (Ackerman, 1992).

Musical Atmosphere

Use music to set a particular mood or mental state and then shut it off when you have accomplished your aim. If you flood the background with music for no purpose, its potential to have an effect on student attention and interest is significantly diminished. Experiment with music to set the stage for specific lessons, activities or even thematic units or transitions between classes.

- To excite students and generate lots of positive energy, play uptempo, upbeat music. Anthologies and collections of golden oldies have a broad appeal; try classic pop tunes like *Pretty Woman* by Roy Orbison or *Brown-Eyed Girl* by Van Morrison.

- If you want to set a quiet and contemplative tone as students enter your room or during a transition, play slow-tempo classical music or music by new age composers like Gary Lamb or Enya.

Why It Works...

There are many ways to use music in class and count-less selections and styles to choose from. Studies have also shown that using classical or meditative music can produce increased levels of melatonin, a neurotransmitter that plays a key role in relaxation, sleep onset, heart rate and blood pressure (Tims et al., 1999). Because of the popularity of the book, The Mozart Effect *(by Don Campbell), many people assume that only music com-posed by Mozart or other classical artists can have an effect on students. Although classical music definitely has its place in the classroom, many other musical gen-res, from pop and rock to folk songs, are appropriate for enhancing a lesson. It just depends on your purpose.*

Musical **Routines**

Using music as a trigger to automate daily classroom rituals and routines can be extremely powerful, motivating and effective. For example, instead of telling students it is time to put away their books for lunch or clean up their workstations after an art lesson, use music to prompt the transition. With practice, students will automatically put their work away, get their lunch boxes and line up at the door when they hear the cue song. Musical cues are fun for students and help reduce your stress as a teacher—at the very least you won't have to raise your voice to be heard above the noise of a class working on projects!

Match musical routines to songs according to lyrics. (Be sure to screen all of a song's lyrics in advance to ensure that the content is appropriate for the context and the age level of the learner.)

■ Alert your class that it's lunch time with *Be Our Guest* from the Disney movie, *Beauty and the Beast*.

■ Accompany students as they move around the room with *Come On Over* by Shania Twain.

■ At the end of the day, send your group home to *So Long, Farewell* from *The Sound of Music*.

■ Greet students as they enter your room each morning with the upbeat and chipper *In the Mood* (by Glenn Miller) to put them in the mood to learn and have fun.

Why It Works...

The power of music in the classroom is profound. Emotionally charged events are better remembered than emotionally neutral events. Music that sends shivers down your spine is accompanied by increases and subsequent decreases in cerebral blood flow to areas of the brain thought to be involved in reward, arousal, motivation and emotion (Blood & Zatorre, 2001). Music has also been found to facilitate studying, test taking and learning tasks that require intense concentration (Botwinick, 1997). The uses of music are still being explored, but the message is clear—if you aren't yet utilizing music in your classroom, you should start!

Seating

■ **Location**—Change the perceived front of the room by teaching from the back of the room (or another location) or by moving the chairs and desks to face that way. The activity, *Location* (page 26), has other suggestions.

■ **Arrangement**—Experiment with how you arrange student seats. Try using only chairs, tables instead of desks, desks in pods or rows, or a U-shaped configuration, to name a few.

■ **How**—Have students sit in unusual ways, like with their non-dominant arm on top, clasping a thumb or crossing one ankle over the other. For some lessons, ask them to sit on the floor, on top of their desks or lie on their stomachs.

Why It Works...

Group seating arrangements can foster important social and peer interactions among students, but traditional seating is more effective for some activities, like concentrated independent learning. Students who switched from group seating to rows or pairs improved their on-task time from 16 to 124 percent (Hastings & Chantrey Wood, 2002). But if collaboration, teamwork, problem solving or community building is the desired outcome of a lesson, group seating is recommended.

Hand & Mouth Fidgets

Provide students with hand and mouth fidgets for an effective kinesthetic state change.

Hand fidgets are small items with interesting textures, like finger puppets, Koosh balls, water worms, gel-filled balls, Slinkys or worry stones, that can be manipulated quietly by the student at his desk. Ideally, students would be allowed to go get a fidget if they felt the need for one. You could make them available in a box or bag in some area of the room.

Mouth fidgets are food items with different tastes and textures that students enjoy. Gum chewing is one example of a mouth fidget. If your environment allows for it, introduce snacks with different tastes (salty, sweet, etc.) and textures (smooth, crunchy, etc.) for a kinesthetic state change that will satisfy the need for oral stimulation many of your students have.

Why It Works...

Some students may need more stimulation, some students less. Hand and mouth fidgets allow students of diverse kinesthetic needs to control and choose the amount and quality of stimulation they receive. Even adults doodle while on the telephone or jingle change in their pocket while having a conversation. The option to choose the amount and type of stimulation they need empowers students; exercising the freedom to take control of their learning environment can have a profoundly positive effect on their enthusiasm and interest in learning.

Visual State Change

Experiment with the amount and quality of visual stimulation that your students receive.

- Change the posters, bulletin boards and displays in your classroom every three to four weeks.

- Occasionally introduce different visual elements into your classroom. Add flowers, unusual objects, some artifacts related to the current unit, thematic posters or holiday decorations when appropriate.

- Investigate the use of props—put on a ball cap when you "recap" information during a lecture or look at the class through a picture frame when you give students "the big picture." Novelty items can help anchor information into students' memories.

Why It Works...

Visual information can have a profound effect on long-term learning. Wise educators take advantage of peripheral visual attention by experimenting with the visual displays in their classroom. All the information in their visual field is sent to the brain and processed. A visual state change can instantly refocus a student's attention and assist with recall. Visual scenes containing an element of surprise are forgotten less often and remembered as colorful, vivid and detailed (Rossiter et al., 2001). Consider this, too: Television advertisements containing humor and an element of surprise are the most memorable (Alden et al., 2000).

Deep Breath (any age)

- Have students stand up and take one or two deep breaths, slowly sitting down on their last exhale.

- Add deep breathing to your classroom rituals. For example, have students take a deep breath every time you turn a page during a reading lesson.

- Add an element of competition: Have students stand up, take two deep breaths and sit down on the last exhale only when they are out of breath. The last student standing wins!

Why It Works...

The average human brain weighs only about three pounds, yet consumes up to twenty percent of the body's energy. It requires lots of oxygen to survive, although it can only store about one second's worth (after six seconds without oxygen, your brain loses consciousness). A deep breath helps deliver richly oxygenated blood to the brain to keep it fully alert and functioning optimally.

Silence (any age)

Introducing new information before previous information has time to be processed and placed into long-term memory can be detrimental to both new and old learning. To solidify new learning at the end of a lesson, have students, without any outside interruptions or distractions, silently sit and think or sit and write about the most important points of what they just learned. Don't play music, don't ask questions, don't make them perform any other activity but silent reflection.

The appropriate length of quiet time depends on the age of your audience. Elementary school students may only be able to sit quietly for a few moments; adult learners may appreciate several silent minutes.

Why It Works...

Our brains need time for unconscious processing. While it is possible for the brain to do two things at once (such as listen to the radio while studying), multitasking diverts energy from the brain in order to block out the distraction. When the brain's attention is divided during the learning of new material, blood flow to the areas of the brain involved in focused attention, including the occipital-temporal, medial and ventral-frontal areas, decreases (Fletcher et al., 1998). Enforcing a few moments of silence can be a welcome change from the hustle and bustle of school, and can also help students consolidate and comprehend new learning.

Teach It Standing (any age)

There is no rule that states students learn best while seated at a desk. But go ahead—break that rule anyway!

- Teach to students or have them give each other feedback while they are standing. This will circulate more blood through their system and send oxygen-rich blood to the brain.

 - Conduct a classroom review while the students are standing.

- During lessons when the entire class is reading from the same book or packet, have students stand for every other page.

Why It Works...

Standing increases blood flow and actually improves the brain's ability to pay attention because it stimulates the body's adrenal glands and pumps adrenaline into the system. (Adrenaline also stimulates the amygdala, the emotional center of the brain.) The role adrenaline plays in enhancing memory was discovered at the University of California at Berkeley (McGaugh et al., 1999). Rats put into water had to swim to find a submerged transparent platform to stand on and rest. Their survival needs triggered a rush of adrenaline into their systems. When the rats were returned to the water after a significant length of time had passed, they easily remembered the location of the platform. Rats given beta-blockers (beta-adrenergic blocking drugs) to neutralize the effect of adrenaline on their amygdala did not remember the location of the platform.

Stand and Stretch (any age)

School chairs are notoriously awkward to sit in—they are designed for efficient stacking, not comfortable learning.

■ Never make students sit for longer than twenty minutes.

■ Play music with a slow tempo and have students stand at their desks and stretch. They don't need to do anything fancy—just reach for the sky or rotate at the waist, whatever their body tells them to do.

■ Put students in small groups and have a volunteer lead a stretch. For tips on how to choose student leaders, see *Choosing Volunteers* (on page 8).

■ Have students do "The Wave" around the classroom. They'll stand up, stretch their arms high and shout, "Whooo!" in a wave-like sequential pattern. (This activity can generate a lot of excitement and enthusiasm, too. Let the wave stay in motion as long as it continues to be a fun and spontaneous activity. Don't worry—it will end itself naturally.)

Model safe and appropriate stretches for your class. Younger students may not be mature enough for the responsibility of small group stretches.

Why It Works...

Sitting in chairs puts enormous pressure on the spine, which will eventually lead students to unconsciously shift and fidget to relieve the tension. An inexperienced teacher may get annoyed at student movement, but it really indicates that students would benefit from the chance to stand and loosen up. Then, the brain can return its full attention to learning.

Pump It Up (any age)

Second only to the heart, the calf muscles are the best pumps the body has for moving blood through the body and energizing the brain.

- Have students stand and do ten to fifteen toe lifts. They can lift up on both feet at once, do one set of lifts on the right foot and then on the left foot, or alternate feet for each lift.

- Have students march in place to John Phillip Sousa's *Stars and Stripes Forever* or the theme from *The Mickey Mouse Club* television show.

- Do "popcorn" lifts. Start very slowly but gradually increase the frequency until students are doing lots of toe lifts in rapid succession. Have them finish by gradually slowing down and finally stopping.

Why It Works...

Because the brain does not store energy, it constantly runs on empty. A fresh supply of blood brings it the oxygen and glucose it needs to operate. If the brain does not have enough energy, students become restless, listless and bored. Even if teachers do not incorporate active exercises into their daily routines, they should still watch students' physiology. Their body language and behavior will alert teachers whenever a quick, energizing activity is needed.

Positive Affirmations

(any age)

In most classrooms, positive affirmations like, "Excellent job," and, "Keep up the good work," are passed only from teacher to student. But imagine a classroom in which the teacher *and* students delivered positive affirmations on a regular basis— this kind of supportive environment can affect students very positively and powerfully.

There are no hard and fast rules for giving out positive affirmations and no set phrases to say.

- At the end of a group or partner exercise, have students exchange positive affirmations.

- Enhance affirmations with physical gestures. Introduce this addition by saying something like, "Turn to your partners, give them high fives and say, 'great ideas,'" or, "Turn to your partner, shake hands and say, 'You're a genius!'" The physical action makes an affirmation easier for a shyer student to give.

■ Tell students to be creative and come up with new gestures to use. Have them invent gestures on the spot or lead a short brainstorming session for ideas that everyone can use.

Model for younger students appropriate ways to give affirmations, perhaps even providing and discussing phrases they could use.

Why It Works...

Affirmations are a wonderful way to facilitate a supportive environment in a classroom. Like many of the activities in this book, they help create an atmosphere of mutual trust and support to counteract the student impulse to "downshift." Downshifting is a biological response of the brain to fear of a perceived threat (Hart, 2002). Students who have downshifted have difficulty focusing on anything not directly related to their survival. Positive affirmations make students feel good not only for receiving praise but for the chance to interact with others in a warm and friendly way.

Meet Three People Who... (upper elementary school to adult)

Have students stand and shake hands with three people who...

- ...are wearing black.

- ...have traveled abroad.

- ...wear a bigger shoe size.

- ...have been on a cruise.

- ...have the same number of siblings as them.

- ...were born in the same month.

- et cetera

Why It Works...

Building community and increasing trust among student groups can help them avoid downshifting (see Positive Affirmations *on page 50 for an explanation of this term). Many of the activities in this book are designed to increase community and bonding between class-mates. For some students, however, these activities may feel threatening or uncomfortable. One way to ease students into these activities is by implementing a* gradient. *To design activities according to a gradient, start off the year with very low-risk activities. When students are more comfortable in the classroom and with each other, raise the gradient slightly and build on previous student suc-cess. Most students will find that* Meet Three People Who... *has a fairly low gradient and therefore will partic-ipate without fear of failure or the sense of taking a personal risk.*

Arm's Length Away

(upper elementary school to adult)

■ Have students stand facing a wall, just close enough so that when they extend their arm straight out towards the wall, their fingertips barely brush it.

■ Without moving away from the wall, have students make a fist with one hand, bend their arm in a right angle, and squeeze and tense their arm muscles for a count of ten.

■ When they are done counting, instructs the students to again reach towards the wall, noting how much shorter their arm has become.

■ Without moving away from the wall, have students relax and shake the tension out of their arm muscles and reach for the wall again. They will notice that the arm has lengthened back to its original size!

■ Repeat the activity on the other arm so students can better observe the changes in their arm muscles and so they don't go back to their seats unbalanced.

Why It Works...

The body responds psychologically and physiologically to both real and perceived threats in the classroom or in life. When threat is perceived, students downshift to the more primitive areas of the brain in control of brute survival and are unable to freely access the neocortex, which is essential for new learning. Arm's Length Away is an activity that can also act as a springboard for many discussions, such as the effect of stress on the body or the physical effect of psychologically tense moments, like when one student has been put down or insulted by another.

Enrolling Questions
(any age)

Enrolling questions are low-threat, easily answered questions presented to the entire group about any topic—that aren't actually questions! They allow everyone to participate without the stress of being put on the spot in front of their peers. These "questions" also eliminate confusion by containing within their syntax directions for how the student should respond. Samples of enrolling questions are listed below.

■ Raise your hand if your eyes are green.

■ Sit down if your shoe size is five or smaller. (You pause.) Sit down if your shoe size is seven or smaller. (Keep going to see who has the largest shoe size in the class.)

■ Please move to the right side of the room if you have ever traveled outside of the country. (Next, find out who has traveled the farthest!)

■ Stand up if you have ever been on a cruise.

■ If you weighed more than seven pounds at birth, stand by the window. (Find out who weighed the most.)

■ Clap your hands if you have ever had a brush with a celebrity or sports star.

The number of siblings, the most pets, favorite dessert... lots of topics are entertaining and of interest to students. Tailor them to suit the age group of your audience. Ask baby boomers where they were during the first moon landing; ask fifth graders if they like to rollerblade. You could even have students brainstorm questions to ask each other—or you! (Wouldn't that be a fun way to introduce yourself and your credentials at the start of a course?)

Why It Works...

Any change, state change or otherwise, includes an inherent risk factor for students. While this risk factor varies greatly with each student, some activities included in this book will be more risky than others. Setting the level of risk very low at the beginning of a school year or course will encourage students to participate. As time passes and they learn more about their classmates and feel more comfortable in the group, they will be likely to try riskier things. Answering enrolling questions is a very low-risk way to participate in class and learn how much they have in common with each other.

Cross Laterals—
Hook-Ups (any age)

Lead the class through a set of *Hook-Ups* postures.

- Stand up and extend your arms in front of you, palms facing each other.

- Bring your palms together until they pass each other and cross at the wrists.

- With your wrists crossed, turn your palms to face each other and interlock your fingers.

- Bring your locked hands in towards your body and turn them so they face up.

- Cross your legs at the knees or ankles.

- Relax your tongue against the roof of your mouth.

- Take three or four deep breaths through your nose.

- Unclasp your hands and shake them out.

- Try this posture in a standing position.

If students, especially young students, find this posture tricky, break it down into crossing just the legs or just the arms until they develop the coordination for it.

Turn *Hook-Ups* into a partner game.

- Partner #1 moves into a standing *Hook-Ups* posture.
- Partner #2 points to one of the first partner's fingers, without actually touching it.
- Partner #1, in the *Hook-Ups* posture, wiggles the finger that Partner #2 is pointing at.
- Point at and wiggle a few more fingers.
- The partners switch roles.

Why It Works...

The book, Brain Gym, *by Paul Dennison and Gail Dennison (Edu-Kinesthetics, 1989) is full of activities designed to increase bilateral processing.* Hook-Ups *is borrowed from this set. Almost 55 percent of students in the third and fifth grades who participated in* Brain Gym *activities for fifteen minutes a day were shown to improve their reading scores on standardized tests (Koester, 2001).*

This original partner game, based on the Brain Gym *posture of the same name, not only achieves cross lateral benefits but is also a low-threat social activity for students.*

Cross Laterals 2– Finger-Thumb (any age)

Play a round of *Finger-Thumb*.

- On one hand, hold up your index finger.

- On the other hand, hold up your thumb.

- Simultaneously switch as fast as you can, so that whichever hand held up the index finger now holds up the thumb and vice versa.

- See which students can switch their fingers and thumbs the fastest.

- Try playing this game standing up.

Why It Works...

Imagine a line going down the middle of your body from your nose to your toes. Activities that visually or kinesthetically cross over this body midline are known collectively as cross lateral activities. Cross laterals can stimulate all four lobes of the brain: the frontal lobe, occipital lobe, parietal lobe and temporal lobe, each of which has specialized functions that are needed for learning. The frontal lobe is used for higher-order thinking, the occipital lobe processes visual information, the parietal lobe relays motor and sensory stimuli, and the temporal lobe processes auditory information. Mostly, though, Finger-Thumb *is just fun to play! Expect students to approach you for days afterwards, showing you how they have mastered this activity.*

Cross Laterals 3— Lazy Eights (any age)

■ Stand up.

■ Extend one arm in front of you with the thumb pointing up (and the other fingers curled toward the palm). Center the thumb in front of your nose.

■ Move your thumb in a large, horizontal figure eight, making sure the pattern crosses at the midline of your body (in front of your nose).

■ Follow the track of the thumb with your eyes and without moving your head.

■ Repeat a few times.

Why It Works...

The two hemispheres of the brain each have specialized functions. The left hemisphere is good at sequencing and recognizing parts; the right hemisphere is good at conceptualizing (seeing the big picture). Fully utilizing each hemisphere's potential will help the brain learn. Brain Gym *activities like* Lazy Eights *improve the communication between hemispheres and benefit the brain as a whole (Dennison & Dennison, 1989).*

Cross Laterals 4– Nose-Ear Switch (any age)

Play a round of *Nose-Ear Switch*.

■ With your left hand, grab your nose.

■ With your right hand, cross in front of your left hand to grab your left ear.

■ Switch so that your right hand grabs your nose and your left hand crosses over the right to grab your right ear.

■ See which students can switch their hands the fastest.

■ Try playing this game standing up.

Why It Works…

Besides guaranteeing a giggle from a group of any age, this particular cross lateral activity serves as an interesting springboard for discussing how to learn a new physical skill. Probably everyone will agree that best way to master it is to start as slowly as you need to in order to have a perfect performance every switch. Then, gradually add speed as your brain figures out the pattern. This discovery will be an excellent way to motivate students struggling with academic ideas later. "Remember when you had such trouble playing Nose-Ear Switch*?" you'll ask them. "Now, look at you go! Schoolwork is the same thing—learning a new skill takes time. You did it once; you can do it again!"*

Cross Laterals 5— Cross Crawl (any age)

- March in place.

- While marching, touch each knee with the opposite hand. When the left knee comes up, tap it with the right hand; when the right knee comes up, tap it with the left hand.

- Modify this activity by "slapping leather." Slowly raise each foot behind you, touching the heel of each shoe with the opposite hand.

Challenge older learners by having them march in place or lift their feet as slowly as possible without losing their balance. Also consider varying the sequence of the pattern; start by raising the right knee in a march and then lifting the left foot behind you, or other combinations.

Why It Works...

This is another activity from Dennison and Dennison's Brain Gym. Cross Crawl *not only increases your students' blood flow, it also increases communication between the two hemispheres of the brain.*

Cross Laterals 6— Gotcha! (any age)

Credit for this cross lateral activity must go to the neurokinesiologist, Dr. Jean Blaydes-Madigan.

- ■ Everyone stands in a tight circle, shoulder to shoulder.

- ■ Put your left hand, palm facing up, in front of the person to your left.

- ■ Next, extend the index finger on your right hand and place it in the palm of the person on *your* right (whose upturned palm is in front of you).

- ■ When the instructor says, "Go," you try to do two things simultaneously: lift your right finger out of the palm of your neighbor's left hand and try to grab with *your* left hand the index finger of the person on your left.

- ■ If you successfully grab your neighbor's right index finger with your left hand, celebrate by cheering and waving your hands in the air.

■ Play several rounds of this game.

■ To vary the rules, cross your arms so that your left hand is palm-up in front of the person on your right and your right hand is crossed over your left arm.

Why It Works...

This game works with small groups of six to eight students, as well as with large groups of several hundred. It works as a community builder, wakes up the audience, provides all the benefits of cross lateral motion and is a lot of fun, too!

Seat Changes (any age)

There are many creative ways to get students from one place to another. For example:

- Give students to the count of ten to gather their books and find a new seat within their row. Later on, give them another count of ten to find a seat in the same row but in a different column.

- Divide the room into four imaginary quadrants. Whenever students return to the classroom after a break (or the next day), require them to sit in a new quadrant.

- Have students take a deep breath and slowly exhale. Then, have them take another deep breath, hold it and find a new seat before they let it out.

 Give students a list of actions to perform before taking a seat. For example, say, "Touch three things that are blue and then sit in the nearest seat," "Shake hands with five classmates and then find a place to sit on the opposite side of the room," or, "Before sitting down, touch one natural object and one man-made object."

- Have students balance a piece of notebook paper flat on their palm, and move as quickly as they can to a new seat without dropping the paper.

- Play musical chairs. Have students walk around the room, or up and down the aisles, until the music stops. Students take the nearest seat and you continue the lesson.

Why It Works...

Since memory is so contextual (dependent on emotion and environment), changing seats can help students' long-term memory. Getting people on their feet to change where they are sitting also provides closure to one lesson or idea before you move on to the next. Finally, the more fun you can have with seat changes, the better a transition it will be; movement wakes you up, silly games and music improve everyone's mood, and novelty and mystery activate the emotional and attentional centers of the brain.

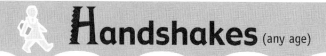Handshakes (any age)

Handshakes change a student's kinesthetic state, as well as increase opportunities for positive affirmations and community building. When students complete an activity, have them shake each other's hands in different ways.

■ Farmer handshakes—One partner (the cow) splays his fingers and the other person (the farmer) "milks" the fingers of his partner's outstretched hand.

■ Fisherman handshakes—One partner extends her hand; the other partner grabs her fingers and winds the thumb of her the hand like a fishing reel bringing in a fish.

■ Shake hands with left hands, pinky fingers or with feet.

■ Alien handshake—With flat, downward-facing palms, partners touch fingertips and wiggle their fingers, making high-pitched sounds like "woogie woogie" or "beep boop bop."

■ Musical handshakes—Partners shake hands normally, but one person squeezes out the rhythm of a familiar song for the other person to guess. They sit down when they have each guessed each other's songs. Songs well suited to this variation include *Twinkle, Twinkle Little Star, Happy Birthday, Row Your Boat* and *Jingle Bells*.

■ Individual students invent their own handshakes and teach them to five other people before sitting down. Alternately, small groups invent a handshake and demonstrate it to the rest of the class before sitting down.

Why It Works...

Social competence is the single best predictor of behavioral success in adulthood (Feehan et al., 1995). Students with antisocial behavior, such as difficulty regulating emotions, maintaining close friendships or acting aggressively, are at greater risk for dropping out of school or developing mental health problems later in life. Early intervention may mitigate some of these problems. In a fun, non-threatening way, activities like Handshakes *can directly and indirectly teach them some of the social skills required to participate in their community.*

Just for Fun

(middle school to adult)

Sometimes you have to do something that is just plain fun! Tell a joke, demonstrate a silly stunt, play a nonsense game or wacky relay race, recite tongue twisters—anything that sparks laughter and encourages hilarity will dramatically improve everyone's mood and make a nice transition into another activity.

Why It Works...

There are psychological and physiological benefits to laughter. Laughter increases the amount of oxygen in the blood, thus stimulating the brain. Intentional humor can also help reduce a sense of threat in the classroom environment. A recent study of three hundred university students found that teachers who used humor in the classroom were perceived as more human, more approachable and more motivating than instructors who did not use humor (Wanzer & Frymier, 1999).

Just for Fun 2—Light a Pickle (middle school to adult)

Warning: This is a stunt for the teacher to do. Do not allow students to try this themselves.

Lighting a pickle actually works. It requires some pre-class, at-home preparation with a few simple tools from a hardware store, but it's worth it. If you have never done this before, you are in for quite a surprise!

■ With a wire cutter, cut off the female end of a small extension cord (like you would use for holiday lights) and strip the plastic back to expose about an inch of bare wire. Carefully separate out two bare wires and thoroughly rewrap the rest of the wires with electrical tape.

■ Wrap each of the bare wires around one 16D nail. Your extension cord should now have a plug at one end and two nails with wire wrapped around them and a bundle of wires wrapped with electrical tape at the other end.

■ Push a nail into each end of a very large dill pickle. *Make sure the nails do not touch!*

■ Turn off the lights in the classroom, hold the pickle with rubber-tipped tongs and plug the extension cord into a regular 110V outlet. Do not touch the nails while the cord is plugged into the wall.

■ Ooh and ahh as you watch the pickle glow.

It may take a few seconds for the pickle to start glowing and may eventually start to smoke or smell, but don't let that stop you from getting the thrill of a lifetime!

(The Brain Store® disclaims any responsibility or liability for damages or injuries that may result from this stunt!)

Why It Works...

Unless you're a science teacher, it will be hard to fit this stunt into your curriculum under any excuse other than having fun! However, the physiological and psychological benefits of laughter a glowing pickle will provoke are well worth the effort of working it into your schedule. Laughter and a good sense of humor have long been known to reduce stress, which decreases the risk of ailments such as heart disease (Crawford, 2000). Intentionally introducing humor in your classroom by telling a joke or plugging pickles into the wall is therefore a good idea!

Just for Fun 3— A Minute of Jokes (any age)

■ After setting the parameters for what constitutes an acceptable joke, give students one minute to share a joke with their classmates at their table or in their group. At the end of the minute, ask student volunteers to share jokes with the rest of the class.

■ Have students prepare a joke in advance for a daily "joke break" ritual. You can assign students to a particular day's break or pull pre-written student jokes out of a box to read aloud.

■ With a partner or in small groups, have students spend a minute relating a funny, unusual or plain-old bizarre personal anecdote. You could have student volunteers share with the entire class some especially interesting stories.

Keep a joke book in the classroom for you to read from or for students to browse so that no one is put on the spot without a joke to tell.

Why It Works...

Telling and understanding a joke involves many parts of the brain, including working memory, cognitive shifting (because jokes require you to look at a familiar thing from a new angle), abstract reasoning and language cognition. Studies have shown that telling or understanding a good joke provides the brain with an invigorating mental workout because all these parts of the brain are stimulated (Shammi & Stuss, 1999).

Additionally, laughter wakes up the brain and the body. A good laugh increases the flow of cerebrospinal fluid throughout the brain and spinal column. The brain releases neurotransmitters that increase your sense of well-being and send "feel good" endorphins to muscle areas, such as the abdomen, neck and shoulders. The combined physiological response to humor helps to relax the body, which in turn influences cognition for the better.

Just for Fun 4—
Student Circus (any age)

Have students think of anything unique they would be willing
to show or demonstrate to the rest of the class, like being
extremely double-jointed, a talent for rolling the tongue, a difficult or popular dance step or the ability to wiggle their ears.
Make a list of volunteers with these unusual abilities and have
them perform whenever a state change is needed throughout
the semester or course.

Why It Works...

Finding something that is unique about a person makes him feel both loveable and capable of achievement—the two foundations of a healthy self-esteem. We know from theories like Gardner's Multiple Intelligences (and from common sense) that each person has different talents to share with the world. Perhaps someone who struggles academically may have incredible kinesthetic intelligence and be able to juggle or walk on her hands. What better, more empowering forum to showcase such a talent than in the positive atmosphere of a supportive classroom?

Musical Tables (any age)

Change sluggish student states to active and alert ones in less than thirty seconds! Simply play some upbeat music and direct students to walk around their tables until the music stops. Or, send students for a walk around the room, media center or gymnasium. If weather and time permit, lead them on a walk around the school playground or parking lot.

If you do not have students seated at tables in your classroom, or if your students are too young to walk around a room without causing disruptions or losing academic focus, have them stay at their desks and dance in place to the beat of the music. Encourage them to dance with lots of enthusiasm. When the music stops, have students freeze like statues. Give them a few minutes to stay in place but look around the room at the silly poses their classmates are in.

Why It Works...

Walking increases oxygenated blood flow to the brain by increasing the rate of blood circulation through the body. Listening to music has been shown to increase spatial reasoning (Rauscher et al., 1993) and may even facilitate focused thinking to enhance general intelligence (Cockerton et al., 1997). Who knew all of these good things could happen just by walking around a table?!

Telling Yarns

(middle school to adult)

■ Greet students at the door with a bundle of yarn and a pair of scissors.

■ As students enter the classroom, cut them a length of yarn as long as they want, but do not tell them what it is for.

■ Seat students in small groups and have them choose a temporary leader.

■ Instruct the group leaders to wrap their piece of yarn around one of their fingers. While they are wrapping the yarn, they share aloud some personal information with their group. Offer some topic suggestions to help them get started; they can talk about how many siblings or children they have, their favorite food or movie or even professional goals and ambitions.

■ When the leader has wrapped the piece of yarn all the way around one finger, the next person in the group takes a turn until everyone has had a chance to participate.

Why It Works...

Students need to learn about their classmates before you can call your classroom a place of community. Sharing personal details is a high-risk activity for some students, but they may be the very students who will benefit the most from the support of an intimate and caring class. Telling Yarns *is a low-gradient activity that reduces the perception of threat and encourages everyone to participate. Holding a piece of yarn that will be used for some unknown purpose draws students in via their curiosity; having yarn to fiddle with as a prop pulls focus from the speaker's words to the speaker's hands, lessening the opportunity for stage fright as well as giving the speaker control over how long he speaks.*

Two Truths and a Lie

(middle school to adult)

■ Put students in small groups and have each person think of two things about themselves that are true and one thing that is untrue. Encourage students to come up with true things that no one in the class could know about or that seem outrageous.

■ In their small groups, students take turn stating, in any order, the two truths and the lie.

■ Group members try to guess which statements are true and which one is false.

Why It Works...

This is yet another activity that provides an opportunity for students to reveal personal information to their classmates in a non-threatening, low-risk environment. Interestingly, scientists at the University of Pennsylvania used fMRI technology (functional magnetic resonance imaging) to show that blood flow increases to different areas of the brain when someone is lying. Subjects who answered questions falsely activated the anterior cingulate gyrus and the left pre-motor cortex regions of the brain, which are responsible for attention, judgment and the correction of errors (Langleben et al., 2001). Hmmm... does this mean a more accurate lie detector is on its way?

Knotty Problem

(middle school to adult)

■ Students form groups of five to eight people and stand shoulder to shoulder in a tight circle, facing inward.

■ Students reach across the circle grabbing hands, reaching for one person with the right hand and another person with the left. There will be a jumble of hands and arms in the middle of the circle.

■ At a signal from the teacher, the groups untie their knots of hands and arms without letting go of each other's hands.

■ When a group successfully unties themselves (they may be in one circle or two smaller, interlocking ones), allow them to celebrate with a cheer and by waving their clasped hands.

Why It Works...

This interactive, highly kinesthetic state changer not only puts students in motion but also gives them an opportunity to team build and practice problem solving, negotiation and communication skills. You'll be amazed by the intensity of students' focus as they maneuver their way out of this tangle.

Life Raft (middle school to adult)

■ Students form groups of five to eight people; give each group an 11" x 14" sheet of construction paper.

■ Groups are challenged to find a way for each of their members to fit onto the paper so that no part of any group member is touching the floor.

■ Groups hold their position until you verify that they have accomplished their goal.

■ When all groups have successfully met this challenge, instruct them to fold the paper in half, short end to short end, and try it again!

■ If time permits, have groups compete to see who can fit on the smallest piece of paper!

(One solution is to have everyone in the group put one foot on the paper, lift the other off the floor and hold onto each other for balance. You'll be stunned by the other creative solutions your students devise.)

Why It Works...

Because of the physical proximity it requires, this team-building activity has a high gradient of stress and perceived risk but it inspires creativity and has a potentially tremendous payoff when the group succeeds (pride of accomplishment, satisfaction of winning or new friends in the class). It is also an excellent enrolling activity for a discussion about changing paradigms, overcoming obstacles and maintaining an optimistic attitude.

Hand Jive
(upper elementary school to adult)

This hand jive is the same one they used to do in the golden age of rock and roll. Any peppy, uptempo piece of music will work as accompaniment, but *Willie and the Hand Jive* (by Johnny Otis) or *Born to Hand Jive* from the soundtrack of *Grease* are both particularly fun to use.

In case you don't know the *Hand Jive*, the motions are listed here. It is a sixteen-beat pattern and moves very fast!

■ Pat your lap twice and then clap twice.

■ With your palms facing down, cross your hands in the air twice. Cross your hands twice in the air again, this time with the other hand on top.

■ Bounce one fist on the other twice. Bounce the fists twice again, this time with the other fist on top.

■ With the right hand, jerk a "hitchhiker" thumb over the right shoulder twice. With the left hand, jerk a "hitchhiker" thumb over the left shoulder twice.

Have individuals or small groups of students invent their own hand jives (always in sixteen-beat patterns) and demonstrate and teach their *Hand Jives* to the rest of the class.

Why It Works...

Movement increases heart rate and circulation and triggers arousal mechanisms. Activities that include spinning and body rotation, like dance moves, may be essential to the formation of critical brain areas responsible for controlling spatial, visual, auditory and motor functions (Palmer, 1980). When dance and movement are used in the classroom, the emotions released stimulate the amygdala, the brain's emotional center, which is important to the memory process. Combining dance, creative movement and fine arts with classroom learning can improve students' self-image, locomotor coordination and stress response. Having students perform their own versions of the Hand Jive *for each other can facilitate the maturation of the brain's cortical systems, by putting them "on stage," even if only for a few moments (Jensen, 2000).*

What Are You Doing? (middle school to adult)

■ Have groups of six to eight people stand in a circle. Ask someone to volunteer to start.

■ The volunteer starts off by pantomiming an easily recognizable activity, such as painting a wall, riding a bicycle or milking a cow.

■ The person to his left asks, "What are you doing?"

■ Without stopping his original pantomime, the first person answers with a second activity. For example, he might answer with the statement, "I'm doing jumping jacks."

■ The second person starts doing the named activity (in this example, jumping jacks). As soon as she begins, the first person stands still.

■ As the second person performs her activity, the person on her left asks, "What are you doing?" and so on.

■ Add another element of challenge by having participants keep up their pantomime even after they've answered the question.

Why It Works...

Multi-tasking is the name of this game! What Are You Doing? *requires participants to be engaged in one activity, think of another activity and ask and answer questions at the same time. The more you can engage the brain in multiple tasks, the more completely you engage and stimulate all four brain lobes. Twice around the circle is an appropriate length of time to play the game—too much longer and students will tire physically and mentally.*

Brave New Words

(middle school to adult)

Display on an overhead transparency or large poster a list of words that describe positive moods (see examples below). Instruct students to choose a word that describes either how they feel or how they want to feel. Then, have students introduce themselves to every other person in the room, using their chosen word in their greeting. For example, I might say, "Hi. My name is Jerry and I'm feeling groovy!"

Some sample words:
groovy, wonderful, magnificent, superb, splendid, glorious, brilliant, outstanding, stupendous, dazzling, sanguine, confident, optimistic, cheerful, ecstatic, blissful, elated, delighted, euphoric, jubilant, astounding, amazing, stunning, spectacular, cool, hip, harmonious, blissful

Take time to quickly go over the definitions of any words, like sanguine, that you think your students may not know. (For the record, sanguine means cheerfully optimistic, hopeful or confident; from the Latin word for "blood"; one of the four Cardinal Humors from the 17th Century —sanguine, phlegmatic, choleric and melancholic.)

Why It Works...

This enjoyable, low-gradient state change is non-threatening yet highly interactive and can help build vocabulary! The social bonding in combination with kinesthetic walking and handshaking make this activity especially good for periods of low energy, like at the beginning of an early class or right after lunch.

Got My Eye on You

(upper elementary school to adult)

■ In groups of six to eight people, students stand in an inward-facing circle and choose a leader, whose job will be to say "go" and keep score.

■ To begin the game, everyone in the circle looks down at the floor.

■ When the leader says, "Go," participants raise their eyes to look at another group member and hold their gaze.

■ If two people have made eye contact with each other, the group gets a point.

■ Continue this game until the group reaches a total of ten points. No fair talking between rounds to arrange who is going to look where—that's cheating!

Use this as a concluding activity before a break or at the end of the day. When a group has reached ten points, they are all dismissed to leave.

Why It Works...

This low-gradient activity encourages non-threatening eye contact, which builds rapport. It is also a low-stress competition, because the only way to score points is with good luck! The most gifted and the most challenged students are on the same playing field and will enjoy playing this activity together. Finally, there is something electrifying about looking up to see someone looking back at you that students of all ages seem to enjoy.

Do Over! (middle school to adult)

In groups of six to eight people, students stand in a circle, facing inward and looking down so that no group member is making eye contact with any other person. Have students count off from one to ten as quickly as possible as they go around the circle. If two people say a number at the same time or if someone's turn is skipped, the next person must start over from one.

Why It Works...

In school and at work, making mistakes is generally looked upon as something to be avoided. However, making mistakes can greatly facilitate learning, if it is handled correctly and used as feedback for the learner. If the learning environment allows for errors, certain types of learners respond better to the learning process (Gully et al., 2002). Specifically, math teachers who emphasized learning and understanding of mathematical concepts rather than performance produced more confident, inquisitive learners that were less afraid of making mistakes and used fewer avoidance strategies to resist learning (Turner et al., 2002). In the game of Do Over!, *students almost always make mistakes as they learn the order of the voices without looking at the faces.* Do Over! *gives students of all abilities the chance to make mistakes and learn from them in an enjoyable, threat-free way, which will hopefully carry over into academic subjects. Savvy teachers will do their best to make sure it does.*

Alphabet Find
(middle school to adult)

■ Put students in pairs or small groups no bigger than four and hand each of them a sheet of paper with the letters of the alphabet written in order, top to bottom.

■ Challenge the groups to see who can think, for each letter, of one thing that they have learned in the course or subject. For example, in a literature class, a group could write "metaphor" for "M."

■ The first group to complete the alphabet, or the group that uses the most letters, wins.

■ Vary the activity by making it a team-building exercise instead of an academic activity. Have the groups find an object for every letter of the alphabet, using only what they have at their desks, including the contents of their purses, pockets, wallets, notebooks and backpacks. Accept any creative answer they can sufficiently justify.

■ At the end of the activity, have group members share a few of the more clever or creative items they came up with.

It would take a long time for all the groups to read all their answers, defeating the purpose and energy of the activity by boring everyone. Instead, give each group an overhead transparency or large piece of paper to write on for display so everyone in the class can read all the lists.

Why It Works...

This activity encourages group members to rely on each other for ideas, creativity and motivation. Having each team share with the whole group what items they used for each letter is a fun way for a group to show off its creativity. Students will also see how much they have in common with each other when they hear that many people found the same solutions to this challenge.

Crowd Pleasers
(high school to adult)

■ The entire class huddles up at the center of an open area. Bring with you a portable CD or cassette player and some upbeat, bouncy, instrumental music.

■ Students drop their heads and hands, keep their eyes on the ground and shuffle around close to each other, snapping their fingers in time to the music.

■ When you pause the music, students stop their shuffling (but do not look up) and wait for instructions.

■ Give the group a task to perform while the music is silent, such as, "touch two pieces of jewelry," "touch two items colored red," "touch a white shoe," "put your right elbow on someone else's knee," or, "put your left hand on some one else's sleeve." They may have to search to find that object or color.

■ Then, turn the music back on and have students again shuffle around, snapping their fingers until you stop the music and give them the next set of instructions.

Why It Works...

Because of its extreme physical proximity, this activity may generate a higher level of stress than other community building exercises. Ease participants into this closeness by starting with generic and less personal instructions ("touch someone else's shoulder" or "touch a white shoe") and replaying the music within a few seconds. As they become more comfortable in the crowd, you can lengthen the pause of music and elaborate on the directions that you give.

Circle Games—
Ooh! Ahh! (upper elementary to adult)

■ The entire class, including the teacher, stands in a circle holding hands.

■ The teacher starts by squeezing the hand of the student on the right and saying, "Ooh!"

■ That student squeezes the hand of the next person on the right and says, "Ooh!"

■ Students pass the squeeze and the "Ooh!" to the right until it comes back to the teacher.

■ Next, the teacher squeezes the hand of the student on the left while saying, "Ahh!"

■ The "Ahh!" squeeze continues around the circle.

■ To make the game more fun on the second round, have a student volunteer start the "Ooh!" squeeze (to the right) while at the same time the teacher starts an "Ahh!" squeeze (to the left). Watch to see where they collide!

Why It Works...

Excessive worry over tests, grades and overall academic achievement can impair both cognition and physical health (Ashcraft & Kirk, 2001). A round or two of Ooh! Ahh! can increase student bonding, thereby lowering the sense of the classroom as a threatening place and improving the environment for learning.

Circle Games 2—
Buzz Fizz (upper elementary school to adult)

■ Have all the students stand in a circle, facing the center, and number off from left to right.

■ Once everyone has a number, add complexity. Have them number off again from the same starting point, except this time, a student says, "Buzz!," when the number is a multiple of three: 1, 2, Buzz!, 4, 5, Buzz!, 7, 8, Buzz!,... (Try using other numbers before moving on to the next step.)

■ Add another level of complexity by introducing a second sound to the counting. For example, use "Buzz!" for multiples of four and "Fizz" for multiples of five: 1, 2, 3, Buzz!, Fizz!, 6, 7, Buzz!, 9, Fizz!, 11, Buzz!,... (If a number is a multiple of both, that student must "Buzz!" and "Fizz!")

■ Experiment with different sound effects, or go around the circle two or three times during the same count instead of stopping it at the first person.

Elementary students may become easily frustrated if two sounds are in play. Use only one sound effect unless the group has really caught on to the rhythm and counting of the activity.

Why It Works...

For two years, teachers in twenty-five schools in four states were studied to determine which teaching practices most impacted test scores (Langer, 2001). One of the findings was that successful teachers used many different approaches to skill instruction, rather than a single drill or lesson format. A game like Buzz Fizz *is one way to bring variety into your classroom as well as stimulate your students' attentional systems, appeal to visual, auditory and kinesthetic learners, and enjoy the peripheral benefit of developing an entertaining, interpersonal classroom environment. This game is also an excellent pick-me-up to help students snap out of a dull or listless state.*

Circle Games 3— Lap Sit (upper elementary school to adult)

■ Have the entire group of students stand in a tight circle, shoulder to shoulder, facing the center.

■ Direct the students to make a quarter turn to the right, so that they now face the back of their neighbor's head and their left shoulders are inside the circle.

■ Now, have everyone gently place both of their hands on the shoulders of the person in front of them.

■ Walk around the circle, encouraging them to make it as tight as possible—they'll need to be very close for the next step!

■ Finally, instruct everyone to slowly sit down on the knees of the person behind them. If the circle seems stable and confident, encourage them to slowly lift their hands in the air and cheer.

■ Remove students from the circle by having them put their hands back on the shoulders of the person in front of them and waiting for your cue so they all stand at once.

■ You can also make this circle in the opposite direction.

Why It Works...

This classic team-building activity works with ten people or several hundred! It is an exceptional springboard for dialogue about teamwork, trust, relying on group members or providing support and cooperation. Social interaction, physical movement and carefully following instructions combine to make this a high-energy, effective kinesthetic state change.

Circle Games 4—Yurt Circle (upper elementary school to adult)

(A *yurt* is a portable dwelling made of branches and felt, used by the nomadic tribes of Mongolia.)

- Have all the students stand in a circle, facing the center, and number off by twos (one-two-one-two, etc.).

- If there is an odd number of participants, the teacher needs to join the group between the first person to count off and the last person. (The teacher's number will be "two.")

- Everyone in the circle holds hands.

- Very slowly, being aware of the changing dynamics of the group, the "ones" slowly lean in toward the center of the circle and the "twos" lean back out of the circle, keeping their feet firmly on the floor.

■ Slowly and fluidly, have everyone rock so that the "ones" are leaning out and the "twos" are leaning in. Switch places a few times so everyone can feel the shift of balance and motion.

For younger students, be sure to introduce this activity with a discussion about safety and the ability to rely on each other for support. Then, give them an idea about how slowly they should either lean in or out—perhaps to a count of three or five. With adults you can just instruct them to lean forward or backward at your signal. You will probably not have to switch places more than once with adults for them to appreciate the experience.

Why It Works...

Research supports the benefit of group-oriented activities. Group activities lead to increased commitment to academic effort and school values (Holloway, 2000). Like Lap Sit, Yurt Circle *can be used as a springboard for a discussion about group dynamics, relying on teammates, trust or cooperation.*

Sculpture Garden

(high school to adult)

■ In pairs, students decide who will be Artist and who will be Clay.

■ The Artists mold their partners, Clay, into any sculpture position they would like, experimenting with form, expression and pose. Encourage as much creativity as possible! When Artist is finished, Clay must stay still, like a statue on display.

■ When all the Clay is sculpted into place, the Artists wander around the "gallery," admiring each other's work.

■ Have partners switch places, so the Artists become Clay and the Clay become Artists.

■ To make this activity even more interactive, have partners form foursomes so two Artists can jointly sculpt two Clays into one larger statue.

Why It Works...

This activity is a wonderful opportunity for the creative student to shine, while still enjoying the experience of bonding with classmates. The more often we can make our classroom environment a place that is challenging but supportive and with a low gradient of threat, the more learning-friendly it will become. Sculpture Garden is fun, but it is also exciting, challenging, creative, friendly and a tiny bit competitive (which artist will sculpt the best statue?)—the perfect environment for spurring students to give a little more effort than usual.

Bumblebee (middle school to adult)

■ Have students sit around a table close enough to each other to easily reach something in front of their neighbor.

■ Have students place in front of themselves an unbreakable object that is easy to grab. A ring of keys or loosely crumpled piece of paper would be appropriate; a pencil or flat sheet of paper would not work well.

■ Students clap, slap and grab in the following sequence, keeping a steady, six-beat rhythm:
1—slap the table top once with both hands
2—clap your hands once
3—slap the table top twice with both hands, quickly
4—clap your hands once
5—reach with your right hand and grab the object in front of the person to your left
6—slide the object in front of you

■ Repeat the pattern. To increase the excitement of the game, gradually speed up the tempo of the pattern once students are comfortable with its motions.

Why It Works...

The repetitive, unison muscle movements of this activity reinforce the fact that students are working together to accomplish a common goal, which stimulates the neurotransmitters in the brain that contribute to feelings of well-being. Furthermore, the activity activates many senses at once, adding to the all-around learning experience. Mostly, though, it prompts laughter and camaraderie, especially once the game starts moving very fast.

Silence Is Golden
(upper elementary school to adult)

Tell students that, without speaking a work or making any other sounds, they must arrange themselves in a line by birthday. Alternately, ask them to arrange themselves by height, in alphabetical order by name (first, last or middle) or by any other condition you can think of!

Why It Works...

Not only does this activity get students out of their chairs and keep them moving in an interactive, unthreatening environment, it provides everyone with personal information about their classmates as well as an extended moment of silence—something quite valuable at certain times of the day! These silent negotiations enable some students to shine with their top-notch non-verbal communication skills, although others may become very frustrated by the absence of verbal communication. Finally, make sure to facilitate student success; as you watch the students attempt to order themselves, look out for participants who do not seem to be having a good time and set them together with those people who have the non-verbal information exchange down pat.

Balloons Up!
(upper elementary school to adult)

■ Students form circles of six to eight people.

■ Everyone in the circle reaches in and grabs the hands of two other people.

■ Toss one or a few balloons (inflated with air, not helium) into each circle; the groups are required to keep the balloons aloft without letting go of each others' hands.

■ Spice up the game by adding rules along the lines of no person is allowed to hit the balloon twice in a row or you must name a fact from the previous lesson each time you hit a balloon.

■ To vary the activity, give students helium balloons and instruct them to keep the balloons from floating to the ceiling, or require that students use any body part other than their hands to keep the balloons in the air.

Why It Works...

Social cooperation is intrinsically rewarding to the human brain (Rilling et al., 2002). Having students participate in group endeavors like Balloons Up! *can help increase their sense of community by emphasizing the group instead of the individual, making the classroom a friendlier, less threatening place to be.*

Hula Hoop Pass

(upper elementary school to adult)

- Students form circles of six to eight people and join hands.

- Give a Hula Hoop to each group and instruct them to pass it around the circle without letting go of hands.

- Make the activity more challenging by giving them two Hula Hoops to pass, in the same or opposite directions.

- Add an element of competition to the activity by racing against the clock or another group.

Why It Works...

This is one of the few state-changing activities in this book that requires a prop. Props can help lower the stress level of students who are shy or uncomfortable in close physical proximity or among relative strangers; having a prop to hold can help them keep their focus on the goal of the activity instead of their anxiety about the immediate environment.

Motion Potion

(upper elementary school to adult)

Because this activity is auditory, visual and kinesthetic, it is an excellent tool for learning and remembering names at the start of a course.

- Have the entire class stand in a circle.

- Going around the circle in turn, students say their name, prefaced by an aptly descriptive adjective with the same beginning sound. As they say their names, students will also make a unique motion with their hands. For example, "Talkative Teresa" might open and close her hands like a duck.

- When a student has said his name, everyone in the circle repeats the adjective and name, and mimics the motion.

Why It Works...

The brain stores information according to different attributes and features. The implication of this fact for teaching is that memories can be stored in multiple ways, in multiple locations. Capitalizing on this ability will later aid in the retrieval of learned information. Motion Potion *is an effective memory tool because it stores each name with a unique sound, sight and physical motion. Often when trying to recall a student's name, your memory of the physical motion or adjective will trigger the memory of the name. Few things can help build rapport quickly in a group better than knowing everyone's name in a group; this activity is silly but it works!*

Hand to Fist

(upper elementary school to adult)

Hand to Fist is like playing a game of "patty-cake" but with a crafty twist.

- In pairs, students stand facing each other.

- Each partner makes a fist with the right hand and holds up the left hand with the palm open and facing the other person.

- Slowly at first, the partners cross and push their hands together so that palm meets palm and fist meets fist. They pull their hands back and switch so that their left hands are now in fists and their right palms face each other. They push their hands together again.

- Building up speed as the game progresses, partners continue to cross and push their palms and fists together, alternating with every contact.

Why It Works...

This game is a great equalizer. It doesn't seem to matter if a student is successful in school or is struggling—any student pair could be the one to catch on first and you won't be able to predict who they'll be! Putting students who may customarily be behind the rest of the class academically in a position to coach their classmates with a task they immediately mastered will give them an opportunity to show off their skills and interact in a new way with their peers. Students will come up to you for days afterward showing you how they have mastered this activity.

String Squares

(upper elementary school to adult)

■ Put students in groups of six to eight people and give each group a length of string or yarn about fifteen feet in length.

■ Have groups make a series of particular shapes—triangle, octagon, six-pointed star or trapezoid, for example—with the string as you call them out. Call out a variety of shapes, even some that have more sides or points than there are people in the group!

■ Require that groups make the shapes with all members holding onto the yarn.

■ Make the activity more challenging by asking students to create the shapes with their eyes shut or without speaking.

Why It Works...

Not only is this activity a team- and community-builder, it makes abstract geometric concepts tangible as students kinesthetically and personally involve themselves in the design of two-dimensional shapes and see the many forms some shapes, like triangles and hexagons, can take. After this tactile experience, more students will be able to transfer abstract learning to the page during assignments or assessments. It will also be interesting for students to experience the group dynamics as natural leaders emerge, as leaders are chosen by group members or as designated, non-volunteers are assigned to the task of leading their peers.

Fast Fingers

(upper elementary school to adult)

■ Students choose a partner and decide who will go first.

■ Partners stand back to back.

■ Give the class a specific math operation, like subtraction or multiplication, to use during the play of this game.

■ The first partner creates a math problem using the designated math operation and displays the problem on the fingers of both hands (you are limited to numbers of five or less; represent zero with a fist). For example, if the game used addition, five fingers held up on one hand and four on the other would signify the addition problem "5 + 4."

■ At your cue, the partners turn around to face each other. The first partner displays the math problem and the second partner must solve it and say the answer within a time limit you set (the time depends on the skill of the participants but should be equal for all). The first partner must verify that it is correct and provide the right answer if it is not.

■ Partners turn back-to-back again and the second partner devises a math problem for the first partner to solve at the next cue.

Why It Works...

Have you ever been driving down the road and suddenly remembered the name of a movie you couldn't remember a few days before? Your problem wasn't storing the information—clearly it was in your brain the whole time—but rather with retrieving it. Experimenting or manipulating new information as you store it in your memory (like by creating math problems on fingers to solve) will encode the data along multiple memory pathways and increase the likelihood that you will be able to retrieve it when you want it. Fast Fingers stimulates and arouses the brain's attentional systems and encodes arithmetic information in three ways: visually, auditorily and kinesthetically.

What's in a Name?

(any age)

Have students stand and balance with one foot slightly out in front of them. Tell them to rotate their foot at the ankle in either direction. As they rotate their foot, challenge them to write their name in the air with their elbow. Vary the activity by writing their name with any body part (perhaps the nose) except the hand, or make the activity more challenging by requiring students to write with one side of the body and rotate the foot on the opposite side.

Young students will probably not be able to balance on one foot while writing their name in the air. Give them some other physical distraction to perform, like shaking their head, bending repeatedly at the knees or sticking their tongue in and out of their mouth.

Why It Works...

This activity is of the rub-your-stomach-and-pat-your-head variety. It arouses and stimulates several areas of the brain, such as the corpus callosum (the band of fibers that connect the hemispheres of the brain), the attentional system and the vestibular system, which keeps tabs on the position and motion of your body through space.

About the Author

Dr. Jerry Evanski has been a teacher and administrator at the elementary, middle and high school level since 1994. He has served on the faculty of several universities, including Oakland University in Rochester, Michigan, teaching courses in leadership, educational philosophy and curriculum development at the undergraduate and graduate levels. Dr. Evanski holds Bachelors and Masters degrees in Music Education and earned his doctorate in General Administration and Supervision from Wayne State University. He is a trained facilitator for SuperCamp, an accelerated learning program that uses cutting-edge research to improve student achievement, and a former presenter at the *Learning Brain Expo*®, a semi-annual conference dedicated to brain-based learning and recent discoveries in brain science. This is his first book for The Brain Store®.

Bibliography

Ackerman, Sandra (1992). *Discovering the Brain*. Washington, DC: National Academy Press.

Alden, D. L., Mukherjee, A., & Hoyer, W. D. (2000). The effects of incongruity, surprise and positive moderators on perceived humor in television advertising. *Journal of Advertising*, 29(2), 1–15.

Allen, Richard (2001). *Impact Teaching: Ideas and Strategies for Teachers to Maximize Student Learning*. Boston, MA: Allyn & Bacon.

Ashcraft, M. H. & Kirk, E. P. (2001, June). The relationships among working memory, math anxiety, and performance. *Journal of Experimental Psychology: General*, 130(2), 224–37.

Berns, G. S., Cohen, J. D., & Mintun, M. A. (1997, May). Brain regions responsive to novelty in the absence of awareness. *Science*, 276(5316), 1272–5.

Blood, A. J. & Zatorre, R. J. (2001, Sept). Intensely pleasurable responses to music correlate with activity in brain regions implicated in reward and emotion. *Proceedings of the National Academy of Science (USA)*, 98(20), 11818–23.

Blaydes-Madigan, Jean (2001). *How to Make Learning a Moving Experience* [videotape]. Richardson, TX: Action Based Learning.

Botwinick, Jill (1997, May). *Developing Musical/Rhythmic Intelligence To Improve Spelling Skills*. Masters thesis, Kean College, Union, New Jersey.

Bischoff-Grethe, A., Martin, M., Mao, H., & Berns, G. S. (2001, Oct). The context of uncertainty modulates the subcortical response to predictability. *Journal of Cognitive Neuroscience*, 13(7), 986–93.

Burns, L. H., Annett, L., Kelley, A. E., Everitt, B. J., & Robbins, T. W. (1996, Feb). Effects of lesions to amygdala, ventral subiculum, medial prefrontal cortex, and nucleus accumbens on the reaction to novelty: Implication for limbic-striatal interactions. *Behavioral Neuroscience*, 110(1), 60–73.

Cahill, L. & McGaugh, J. L. (1998, July). Mechanisms of emotional arousal and lasting declarative memory. *Trends in Neurosciences*, 21(7), 294–9.

Cockerton, T., Moore, S., & Norman, D. (1997, Dec). Cognitive test performance and background music. *Perceptual and Motor Skills*, 85(3 Pt 2), 1435–8.

Connor, J. R. & Diamond, M. C. (1982). A comparison of dendritic spine number and type on pyramidal neurons of the visual cortex of old adult rats from social or isolated environments. *The Journal of Comparative Neurology*, 210, 99–106.

Crawford, B. (2000, Nov 15). Laughter is good for your heart, according to a new University of Maryland Medical Center study. Retrieved September 17, 2003, from University of Maryland Medicine website: www.umm.edu/news/releases/laughter.html

Daylighting in schools: An investigation into the relationship between daylighting and human performance. (1999, August 20). In, *Pacific Gas and Electric Company Report* (pp. 24–9). Fair Oaks, CA: Heschong Mahone Group.

Dennison, Paul & Dennison, Gail (1989). *Brain Gym*. Ventura, CA: Edu-Kinesthetics.

DePorter, Bobbi & Hernacki, Mike (1992). *Quantum Learning: Unleashing the Genius in You*. New York, NY: Dell Publishing.

Diamond, Marian & Hopson, Janet (1999). *Magic Trees of the Mind: How to Nurture Your Child's Intelligence, Creativity, and Healthy Emotions from Birth through Adolescence*. New York, NY: Plume.

Feehan, M., McGee, R., Williams, S. M., & Nada-Raja, S. (1995, May). Models of adolescent psychopathology: Childhood risk and the transition to adulthood. *Journal of the American Academy of Child and Adolescent Psychiatry*, 34(5), 670–9.

Fletcher, P. C., Shallice, T., & Dolan, R. J. (1998, July). The functional roles of prefrontal cortex in episodic memory. I. Encoding. *Brain: A Journal of Neurology*, 121(Pt 7), 1239–48

Gage, F. H., Kempermann, G., Palmer, T. D., Peterson, D. A., & Ray, J. (1998, Aug). Multipotent progenitor cells in the adult dentate gyrus. *Journal of Neurobiology*, 36(2), 249–66.

Goetz, E. T. & Sadoski, M. (1996). Imaginative processes in literary comprehension: Bringing the text to life. In R. J. Kreuz & M. S. MacNealy (Eds.), *Empirical Approaches to Literature and Aesthetics* (pp. 221–40). Norwood, NJ: Ablex Publishing.

Gully, S. M., Payne, S. C., Kiechel Koles, K. L., & Whiteman, J. A. (2002, Feb). The impact of error-training and individual differences on training outcomes: An attribute-treatment interaction perspective. *Journal of Applied Psychology*, 87(1), 143–55.

Guy, S. C. & Cahill, L. (1999, Mar) The role of overt rehearsal in enhanced conscious memory for emotional events. *Consciousness and Cognition*, 8(1), 114–22.

Hart, Leslie (2002). *Human Brain and Human Learning (3rd edition)*. New York, NY: Books For Educators.

Hastings, Nigel & Chantrey Wood, K. (2002). *Re-Organizing Primary Classroom Learning*. Buckingham, United Kingdom: Open University Press.

Holloway, John (2000). Extracurricular activities: The path to academic success? [online]. *Educational Leadership*, 57(4).

James, William (1992). In Gerald Myers (Ed.), *William James: Writings 1878–1899: Psychology, Briefer Course/The Will to Believe/Talks to Teachers and Students/Essays*. New York, NY: Library of America.

Jensen, Eric (2000). *Learning with the Body in Mind*. San Diego, CA: The Brain Store®.

Klein, H. J. & Kim, J. S. (1998, Feb). A field study of the influence of situational constraints, leader-member exchange and goal commitment on performance. *Academy of Management Journal*, 41, 88–95.

Koester, C. (2001). The effect of Brain Gym on reading abilities. Retrieved September 12, 2003, from the Brain Gym website: www.braingym.org/cecilia.html

Langer, Judith A. (2001, Sept). Succeeding against the odds in English. *English Journal*, 91(1), 37–42.

Langleben, D. D., Austin, G., Krikorian, G., Ridlehuber, H. W., Goris, M. L., & Strauss H. W. (2001, Dec). Interhemispheric asymmetry of regional cortical blood flow in prepubescent boys with attention deficit hyperactivity disorder. *Nuclear Medicine Communications*, 22(12), 1333–40.

McGaugh, J. L., Cahill, L., & Roozendaal, B. (1996, Nov). Involvement of the amygdala in memory storage: Interaction with other brain systems. *Proceedings of the National Academy of Science (USA)*, 93(24), 13508–14.

Miles, J. A. & Klein, H. J. (1998). The fairness of assigning group members to tasks. *Group and Organization Management*, 23, 71–96.

Palmer, L. (1980). Auditory discrimination development through vestibulo-cochlear stimulation. *Academic Therapy*, 16(1), 55–70.

Rauscher, F. H., Shaw, G. L., & Ky, K. N. (1993, Oct). Music and spatial task performance. *Nature*, 365(6447), 611.

Rilling, J. K., Gutman, D. A., Zeh, T. R., Pagnoni, G., Berns, G. S., & Kilts, C. D. (2002, July 18). A neural basis for social cooperation. *Neuron*, 35(2), 395–405.

Rossiter, J. R., Silberstein, R. B., Harris, P. G., & Nield, G. (2001, Mar). Brain-imaging detection of visual scene encoding in long-term memory for TV commercials. *Journal of Advertising Research*, 41(2), 13–21.

Shammi, P. & Stuss, D. T. (1999, Apr). Humour appreciation: A role of the right frontal lobe. *Brain*, 122(4), 657–66.

Sousa, David (2001). *How the Brain Learns (2nd edition)*. Thousand Oaks, CA: Corwin Press.

Sturm, Brian. (1999). The enchanted imagination: Storytelling's power to entrance listeners [online article]. *School Library Media Research*, 2. Retrieved September 15, 2003, from the American Library Association website: www.ala.org/Content/NavigationMenu/AASL/Publications_and_Journals/School_Library_Media_Research/Contents1/Volume_2_(1999)/vol2_sturm.htm

Thompson, R. F. & Kim, J. J. (1996, Nov 26). Memory systems in the brain and localization of a memory. *Proceedings of the National Academy of Science (USA)*, 93(24), 13438–44.

Tithof, W. (1998, May). The effects of full spectrum light on student depression as a factor in student learning. Doctoral thesis, Walden University, Minneapolis, Minnesota.

Tims, F., Clair, A. A., Cohen, D., Eisdorfer, C., Koga, M., Kumar, A., Kumar, M., McKinney, C., & Seiger, A. (1999). *Music Medicine: Enhancing Health through Music* (symposium held April 23, 1999, in Miami, FL).

Turner, J. C., Midgley, C., Meyer, D. K., Gheen, M., Anderman, E. M., Kang, Y., & Patrick, H. (2002). The classroom environment and students' reports of avoidance strategies in mathematics: A multimethod study. *Journal of Educational Psychology*, 94(1), 88–106.

Van Praag, H., Christie, B. R., Sejnowski, T. J., & Gage, F. H. (1999a, Nov 9). Running enhances neurogenesis, learning and long-term potentiation in mice. *Proceedings of the National Academy of Science (USA)*, 96(23), 13427–31.

Van Praag, H., Kempermann, G., & Gage, F. H. (1999b, Mar). Running increases cell proliferation and neurogenesis in the adult mouse dentate gyrus. *Nature Neuroscience*, 2(3), 266–70.

Wanzer, Melissa Bekelja & Frymier, Ann Bainbridge (1999). The relationship between student perceptions of instructor humor and students' report of learning. *Communication Education*, 48(1), 48–62.

Woodcock, E. A. & Richardson, R. (2000, Jan). Effects of environmental enrichment on rate of contextual processing and discriminative ability in adult rats. *Neurobiology of Learning and Memory*, 73(1), 1–10.

Learn from Top Education Experts at Learning Brain Expo

The Brain Store hosts Learning Brain Expo, a biannual brain and learning conference for educators and administrators. Visit **www.brainexpo.com** to find out how you can

- ■ boost student achievement through applied brain research
- ■ bridge the gap between neuroscience and the classroom
- ■ translate research into real learning solutions
- ■ learn strategies to help every learner succeed
- ■ earn CEU and graduate credit

Stay up to date!

Visit **www.thebrainstore.com** and sign up for Growing Minds Monthly to get practical, research-based teaching tips delivered right to your inbox!

Are Your Students Driving You Crazy?

Find Out How the Latest Brain Research Can Help You Reach More Students (with Less Stress!)

Resources for Growing Minds ®

Discover Other Great Research-Based Resources from The Brain Store

The Brain Store provides teachers, school administrators, and trainers with resources on the science of teaching and learning made practical.

The Brain Store was the first company to publish and distribute books, music CDs, audio workshops, and other resources that translate the latest discoveries in brain research into practical teaching strategies. The Brain Store's research-based teaching resources are developed by leading education experts and neuroscientists. Request a catalog by calling toll-free at **800-325-4769** or visit the online store at **www.thebrainstore.com**.

Best-Selling Titles *from* **The Brain Store**

Resources for Growing Minds ®

Cognitive Nourishment
Life-Changing Affirmations for the Savvy Teacher
By Louise A. Chickie-Wolfe, PhD

Research has long supported affirmations as a powerful tool to guide the brain toward positive thinking. This little book will inspire a new commitment to excellence for everyone who reads it—refueling and rejuvenating veteran teachers and guiding and reassuring new ones. The inspirational affirmations within will boost the confidence, enthusiasm, knowledge, and pride of anyone involved in the dynamic interactions of education.

©2005 • 96 pages • #1002

Write Brain Write: Proven Success Tools for
Developing the Writer in Every Student
By Anne Hanson

When it comes to teaching writing, what should educators know about the brain and learning? This valuable resource will help you develop effective and passionate student writers in classrooms of any type at any level. From descriptive and narrative writing techniques to expository and persuasive writing strategies, Anne Hanson advocates a "coaching" approach—a quarter-by-quarter game plan that addresses planning, assessment, and curriculum selection. Learn why seating matters, how to think outside the textbook box, what significant changes impact present-day learners' brains, how tapping into the past fuels the fires of the mind, and which real-life applications ensure progress. Develop a classroom full of brilliant writers with this proven, effective approach! ©2002 • 215 pages • #1416

To order these best-selling titles or other brain-compatible learning resources, request our **FREE** catalog. Call The Brain Store at (800)325-4769 or (858)546-7555. Or, visit **www.thebrainstore.com** and browse our online catalog.